Dear Family,

What's the best way to help your child love reading?

Find good books like this one to share—and read together!

Here are some tips.

●**Take a "picture walk."** Look at all the pictures before you read. Talk about what you see.

●**Take turns.** Read to your child. Ham it up! Use different voices for different characters, and read with feeling! Then listen as your child reads to you, or explains the story in his or her own words.

●**Point out words as you read.** Help your child notice how letters and sounds go together. Point out unusual or difficult words that your child might not know. Talk about those words and what they mean.

●**Ask questions.** Stop to ask questions as you read. For example: "What do you think will happen next?" "How would you feel if that happened to you?"

●**Read every day.** Good stories are worth reading more than once! Read signs, labels, and even cereal boxes with your child. Visit the library to take out more books. And look for other JUST FOR YOU! BOOKS you and your child can share!

The Editors

Daddy. . . . Every day,
I try to "remember the good things."
—KR

This book is dedicated to the two most precious people in my life—
my daughter Erica and my nephew Anthony.
—VDH

Text copyright © 2004 by Karla Roberson.
Illustrations copyright © 2004 by Vanessa D. Holley.
Cover illustration copyright © 2004 by Sylvia Walker.
Produced for Scholastic by COLOR-BRIDGE BOOKS, LLC, Brooklyn, NY
All rights reserved. Published by SCHOLASTIC INC.
JUST FOR YOU! is a trademark of Scholastic Inc.

Library of Congress Cataloging-in-Publication Data

Roberson, Karla.
    My shoelaces are hard to tie! / by Karla Roberson ; illustrated by Vanessa D. Holley.
      p. cm.—(Just for you! Level 1)
    Summary: A young girl gets help from her big brother while learning to tie her shoelaces.
    ISBN 0-439-56869-2
    [1. Shoelaces--Fiction. 2. Brothers and sisters—Fiction. 3. Perseverance (Ethics)—Fiction. 4. Stories in rhyme.] I. Holley, Vanessa, ill.
  II. Title. III. Series.
    PZ8.3.R5294My 2004
    [E]—dc22
                                                      2004004773

10 9 8 7 6 5   06 07 08
Printed in the U.S.A. 23 • First Scholastic Printing, April 2004

My Shoelaces Are Hard to Tie!

by Karla Roberson
Illustrated by Vanessa D. Holley

Cover Illustration by Sylvia Walker

JUST FOR YOU!™
Level 1

My shoelaces
are hard to tie.

I have to give it
one more try.

My smart big brother
shows me how.

You can do it.
You try now!

It's as easy as
one, two, three!

Soon, you'll tie them
better than me.

I'll try again.
I'll make a start.

Now here it comes—
the hardest part.

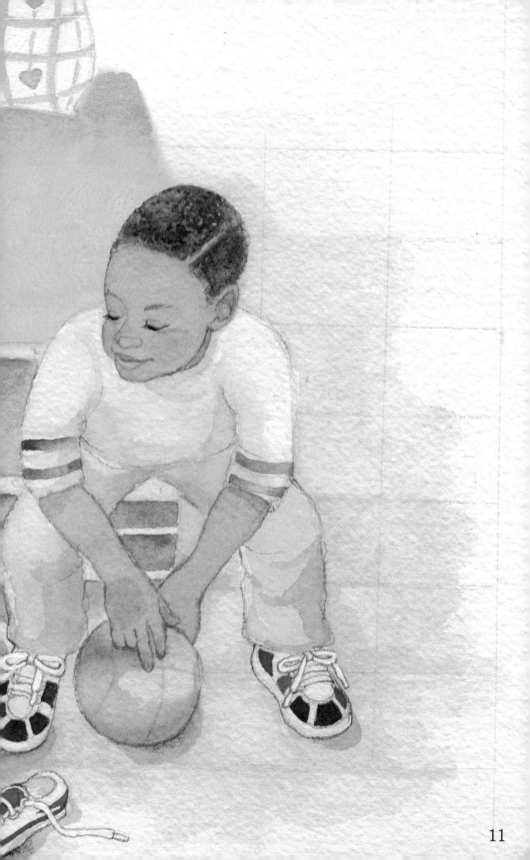

I have one shoelace
nicely looped.

That's hard work—
I'm really pooped!

I bring the other
lace around.

Now my first loop
can't be found!

I give a pull.
I give a tug.
Now my shoelaces
are on the rug!

My shoelaces are
hard to tie!

I can't give up.
I have to try!

My brother smiles.
He'll help me out.

It's okay, Sis.
No need to pout.

I will show you
one more time.

But if you can't,
it's not a crime.

Lace over lace with loops—make two.
Now there's a bow tie on your shoe!

"I tied my shoe!"
I shout with glee.

"All right!" says Brother,
and he high-five's me.

My shoelaces **were** hard to tie.
Now I can do it
each time I try.

"What a big girl!"
say Mom and Dad.
I knew they would
be very glad.

▲▲▲▲▲ JUST FOR YOU ▲▲▲▲▲

Here are some fun things for you to do.

Try, Try Again

It takes hard work
to learn new things.

Think of a time when
YOU had to work hard
to learn something new.

What did you learn?
Did you try and try?
Did anyone help YOU?

Write a story about how you tried and tried.
You can call YOUR story "Try, Try, Again!"

Helping Hands

Why do YOU think
the boy in the story
helps his sister?

How do you think
he felt when she
tied her shoelaces?

Was he proud?
Was he happy?

Can YOU do some things very well?
Make a list of things YOU could help someone learn.

Shout With Glee!

The girl in the story shouts with **glee**!
She is glad that she can tie her shoelaces.

People shout with glee when they are very happy.
What would make YOU shout with glee?

Draw a picture to show what it is.
Draw YOURSELF looking very happy!

▲▲▲▲TOGETHER TIME ▲▲▲▲

Make some time to share ideas about the story with your young reader! Here are some activities you can try. There are no right or wrong answers!

Talk About It: Do you remember how *you* learned to tie your shoes? Or how you learned to read, or write, or ride a bike? Tell your child a story about something you learned to do when you were his or her age. Encourage questions when you are finished with your story. Talk about how it feels to work hard and learn something new.

Think About It: Ask your child, "What if the girl did not have a big brother? Who else could she have asked for help?" The two of you might make a list of people in your family or community who can help children learn new things.

Read It Again: Read the story aloud together, this time stressing the rhyming words. Then play a rhyming game! How many words can the two of you think of that rhyme with *tie, rug, shoe,* and *glad*? See who can come up with the most rhyming words—and have fun doing it!

Meet the Author

KARLA ROBERSON says, "In writing this story, I wanted to tap into my own sense of determination when I was a little girl and use it to encourage children who are going through similar developmental stages. Learning how to tie our shoelaces is something we all must do at a relatively young age. It is one of those rites of passage that gives us our first taste of independence. The main character mirrors my own fierce will as a young girl. To bask in the bragging rights that came along with mastering such a task was great!"

Karla Roberson was born and raised in Oakland, California. She left home to attend college at Howard University in Washington, DC. After graduating, she worked in the Washington area for several years, then relocated to New York City, where she lives today. Karla has worked in publishing and is now a freelance writer. This is her first children's book.

Meet the Artist

VANESSA D. HOLLEY says, "I can remember loving to draw from the time I was three years old. My mother would draw an object on a piece of paper and I would copy it. As I grew older, while other children stayed up late on weekends watching television, you could find me at the kitchen table, creating my own worlds through my drawings."

With no formal art training prior to college, Vanessa applied to the Pratt Institute in Brooklyn, New York, and was accepted. While studying there, she worked part-time as a layout artist and illustrator for *Encore* magazine. Vanessa has illustrated three books to date, including *The Black Holocaust for Beginners* by S.E. Anderson; *Jazz for Beginners* by Ron David; and *Kai: A Mission for Her Village* by Dawn C. Gill, in the Girlhood Journeys series. Vanessa lives with her family in New Jersey.